TRUE CRIME

DNA EVIDENCE

T. R. Thomas

TRUE CRIME

SADDLEBACK
EDUCATIONAL PUBLISHING

www.sdlback.com

ISBN-13: 978-1-59905-438-4
ISBN-10: 1-59905-438-8
eBook: 978-1-60291-764-4

15 14 13 12 11   1 2 3 4 5

Photos:
Kirk Bloodsworth, Andrew Lichtenstein/Sygma/Corbis
Huntsville, Texas, Greg Smith/Corbis
Debbie Smith, Congressional Quarterly/Getty Images

CONTENTS

INTRODUCTION

DNA makes up the building blocks of life. The letters stand for *deoxyribonucleic acid.*

DNA acts like a person's blueprint, or map. Each cell in our body contains our unique DNA. That includes our blood, saliva, hair, skin, muscles, and bones.

DNA profiling was perfected in the late 1980s. The term refers to testing DNA to see if it belongs to a particular person. DNA profiling is also known as *genetic fingerprinting.* Like our fingerprints, each person's DNA is unique. DNA profiling is helpful in solving crimes. It is very accurate.

In 1998 the FBI started operating a national DNA database. The database contains DNA profiles collected by crime labs. Police compare crime scene DNA samples to the database. When they find a match, it often helps solve a crime.

DNA profiling has also been used to free innocent prisoners. DNA testing has *exonerated*, or cleared, more than 200 inmates. Kirk Bloodsworth was the first death row DNA *exoneree*. He was freed in 1993 after spending nine years in prison.

Life can be hard for exonerees. After being in prison, they have a hard time finding jobs and housing. The Innocence Project helps. It also educates people about flaws in the justice system.

CHAPTER 1

DNA PROFILING

DATAFILE

TIMELINE

April 25, 1953

Watson and Crick publish their DNA model.

November 6, 1987

Tommy Lee Andrews is the first U.S. defendant convicted by DNA evidence.

March 12, 2003

Josiah Sutton of Texas is released from prison after being convicted by a faulty DNA test.

Where is Cambridge, England?

KEY TERMS

chromosome—a threadlike body that carries genes

gene—the basic physical unit of heredity

genome—the full set of all the genetic traits people can inherit

helix—a three-dimensional spiral

infallible—absolutely sure or trustworthy

DID YOU KNOW?

Rosalind Franklin took X-ray pictures of DNA in the 1950s. Her work was crucial to the mapping of DNA. Franklin died of cancer at age 37 in 1958. Too much X-ray radiation may have been a factor.

DNA PROFILING

The year was 1953. Scientists James D. Watson and Francis Crick worked feverishly in their lab in Cambridge, England. Watson was American. Crick was British. They were putting together a model of DNA. That stands for deoxyribonucleic acid.

DNA looks like a twisted ladder. Watson called it a "double *helix*." He later published a very famous book called *The Double Helix*. It was about discovering the DNA model.

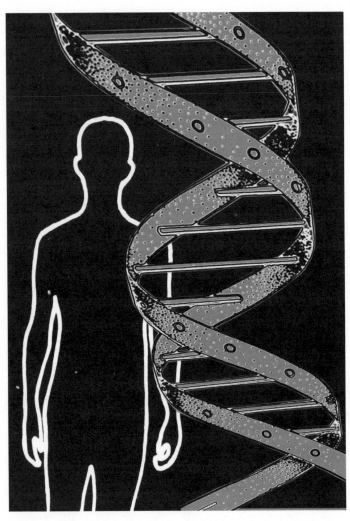

DNA looks like a twisted ladder. Watson called it a "double helix."

Meanwhile, Rosalind Franklin took X-ray photos of microscopic DNA. She was another respected British scientist. Her photos helped Watson and Crick develop their DNA model. Later, in 1962, Watson, Crick, and Maurice Wilkins won the Nobel Prize for their research. Franklin died in 1958, so she could not win.

Earlier scientists had known about DNA. But they didn't understand its structure. And they didn't know exactly what it did.

The Human Genome Project

It wasn't until 2003 that scientists completely mapped DNA. This was the result of the Human *Genome* Project. It was a major milestone in scientific history. Computers played a big role in this complex task.

The Human Genome Project began in 1990. In the beginning, Watson headed the project. He left in 1992 due to conflicts.

Every human has 23 pairs of *chromosomes*. Chromosomes are threadlike bodies. They are made up of DNA and proteins. DNA is made up of *genes*. Each human cell contains three billion DNA base pairs. They make up a very complex pattern. It's what makes us who we are.

Genetic Fingerprinting

Each person's DNA is unique. No two people have exactly the same DNA. Even identical twins' DNA is slightly different. They have the same *genotype*, but the *phenotype* is different. The phenotype is what makes our fingerprints. DNA tests only look at the genotype. A DNA test couldn't tell one identical twin from the other. But their fingerprints would still be different.

Other than that, DNA evidence is more accurate than fingerprints. DNA is found in every cell in our bodies. There doesn't have to be much of it to be tested. Scientists can look at saliva from a cigarette butt under a microscope. DNA from the saliva can tell us who it came from.

DNA testing helps solve crimes. It is extremely accurate. But it is not 100 percent *infallible,* or foolproof. Scientists must perform the test correctly. They also must handle the samples properly. Otherwise a sample could be mislabeled. It could be identified as coming from a different person. Unfortunately, sometimes this happens.

A Bad Junior High Science Project

Houston teen Josiah Sutton was the victim of bad science. In 1998, at age 16, police arrested him for a crime he didn't commit.

But a DNA test showed he was guilty. It took the jury less than two hours to decide the case. The court sentenced Josiah to 25 years in prison.

Three years later, TV reporters got a tip. It was about problems at the Houston police crime lab. The reporters investigated. They sent reports from the Houston lab to experts at a California university. The experts looked over the reports. They were full of errors. One professor said the reports looked like a bad junior high science project.

Luckily, Josiah's mother Batie watched the news that night. It was the answer to her prayers. She contacted the reporters. Eventually the Houston police crime lab was shut down. Josiah Sutton was released from prison. By then he had already been in jail for more than four years.

The First DNA Conviction

In 1987, a British scientist named Alec Jeffreys invented a new test. He called it *DNA fingerprinting.* But forensics scientists didn't like that name. They thought it was too confusing. Today it's usually called *DNA profiling* or *DNA typing.*

Jeffreys used the new test to help solve a murder case. Two young women had been raped and murdered in Leicestershire, England. Police asked men from ages 17 to 34 to submit blood samples. After several months, police had tested more than 4,000 men. The police were about ready to give up. Then they caught a break.

A baker named Colin Pitchfork had asked someone else to take his blood test for him. Police investigated. Pitchfork confessed to the murders. He was the first person ever convicted by DNA typing.

Around that same time, the test was introduced in the United States. The first U.S. defendant convicted by DNA profiling was a Florida rapist. His trial took only three days. The court sentenced Tommy Lee Andrews of Orlando to 22 years in prison.

The trial caused a sensation. There was a media blitz about this exciting new DNA testing. It held a lot of promise. And it has largely delivered on that promise.

DATAFILE

T I M E L I N E

1998

The FBI's CODIS database of DNA profiles begins operation.

October 30, 2004

The Debbie Smith Act is signed into law.

July 17, 2006

Familial DNA testing catches the Shoe Rapist.

Where is Williamsburg, Virginia?

17

KEY TERMS

CODIS—Combined DNA Index System

database—a large, searchable collection of data, or information, kept in a computer

familial—relating to family members

rape kit—a collection of evidence from a rape

suspect—a person the police think may have committed a crime

DID YOU KNOW?

The 1997 movie *Gattaca* starred Ethan Hawke. It was about a future when DNA determined destiny. Hawke's character had inferior DNA. He worried about being found out. He asked, "How can you hide when we all shed 500 million cells a day?"

THE FBI'S DNA DATABASE

Debbie Smith was kidnapped on March 3, 1989. Her husband, a police officer, was asleep upstairs. The intruder broke into their home in Williamsburg, Virginia. He dragged Debbie into the woods and raped her.

The rapist told Debbie to keep her mouth shut. He said he'd kill her or hurt her family if she talked. But Debbie was brave. She told her husband. He drove her to the station. She reported the crime.

Debbie Smith listens during a senate hearing on the Advancing Justice Through DNA Technology Act of 2003. DNA testing identified her attacker.

Doctors collected a *rape kit*. Forensics doctors and nurses examined Debbie. They took photographs of any bruises or other marks. They preserved evidence. They took samples of any fluids, hair, or skin left by the rapist.

Debbie lived in fear for the next six years. The rapist knew who she was. He knew where she lived. He had threatened to kill her if she talked.

The Debbie Smith Act

Finally, after six years, police found the rapist. He was already in prison for other crimes. They found him through the FBI's DNA *database*. He would be in prison for the rest of his life. Debbie and her family breathed a huge sigh of relief. Their six-year wait was over. But they also wondered why it took so long.

Ideally rape kits should be processed right away. They should be compared to the FBI database. If a match is found, police can charge the rapist. In real life this doesn't always happen. Forensics labs lack money for DNA testing. They don't have enough trained staff. So rape kits collect dust on the shelves. And rape victims wait—and worry.

The Debbie Smith Act is changing all that. This law provides money for forensics labs. They use the money to test DNA. It also helps pay for training new staff.

The act went into effect in 2004. Since then, hundreds of rapists have been found. Their victims finally have peace.

CODIS: The Master Key

The FBI's DNA database is called the Combined DNA Index System, or *CODIS*. It began operating in 1998. CODIS includes

DNA profiles of convicted felons. Every state has its own database. CODIS links them all together.

Besides convicted felons, CODIS contains DNA profiles from crime scenes. It also contains missing persons' DNA. Investigators collect DNA at the crime scene. Then they label the results with the date and location. Detectives don't know whose DNA it is. But they know the DNA belongs to whoever committed the crime.

Often criminals commit other crimes. When convicted, their DNA profile goes into CODIS. The computer compares it to other profiles. Sometimes CODIS will find a match with DNA from an unsolved case. That's similar to what happened in Debbie Smith's case.

CODIS helps in missing persons cases, too. When a person goes missing, police add that person's DNA profile to CODIS.

When police find an unidentified body, they test the DNA. If it matches, the victim is identified. These tests help solve cold cases.

CODIS makes it easier to catch serial criminals, too. Serial criminals keep repeating the same crime. Police have caught serial rapists and serial killers with help from CODIS.

Privacy Rights Issues

CODIS creates some privacy issues, however. One question is whether arrest-ees should be included. They have not been convicted. Their guilt has not been proven. Should DNA profiles of innocent people be included in the database? That issue is still being debated.

Another concern is whether *familial* testing should be allowed. That means looking in the database for similar profiles. Blood relatives have very similar DNA.

Let's say a crime is committed. The police collect crime scene DNA. They have a *suspect*. That's someone they think may have done the crime. They compare the suspect's DNA to the crime scene DNA. It's not an exact match.

Next, they look in CODIS. There they find some similar DNA. It could be DNA from the suspect's brother, sister, father, or mother. Police then compare the relative's DNA to the crime scene DNA. If there's a match, police charge the relative with the crime.

The Shoe Rapist

Some people believe the courts should not allow familial testing. That, too, is still being debated in the United States. In England, the courts do allow familial testing. Police have caught several rapists and murderers that way.

DNA EVIDENCE

One British man was known as the Shoe Rapist. Between 1983 and 1986 he raped a number of women. He attacked women walking alone. The women were wearing high-heeled shoes. He would tie them up and rape them. Then he'd take their shoes. Police didn't catch him until 20 years later.

In 2006, police analyzed DNA collected from the rapes. They compared it to the British version of CODIS. There was no match. But they did find some similar DNA. It was from a woman who had a drunk driving violation.

Police asked if she had a brother. She did. The brother was a print shop manager in Rotherham, England. His name was James Lloyd. He was married with children. He had no criminal record. Everybody thought he was a fine, upstanding citizen.

THE FBI'S DNA DATABASE

Police went to talk to him. He broke down. He confessed to four rapes and two attempted rapes. He led police to a secret spot in his office. In it were more than 100 pairs of high-heeled shoes.

CHAPTER 3

KIRK BLOODSWORTH: FIRST DNA EXONEREE

DATAFILE

T I M E L I N E

March 8, 1985

The court sentences Kirk Bloodsworth to death for the rape and murder of a little girl.

June 28, 1993

Bloodsworth is released after DNA testing proves his innocence.

September 5, 2003
DNA proves the identity of the real killer, Kimberly Shay Ruffner.

Where is Rosedale, Maryland?

K E Y   T E R M S

circumstantial—indirect, or of less importance

exculpatory—tending to clear of fault or guilt; usually describes evidence that proves someone innocent

exonerate—to officially clear someone of guilt or blame *after* he or she is convicted of a crime

exoneree—one who has been exonerated

misidentification—to identify someone incorrectly

DID YOU KNOW?

Kirk Bloodsworth's death row cell was right below the gas chamber. Guards once made him paint the gas chamber. They told him to make it "look pretty" for his execution.

KIRK BLOODSWORTH: FIRST DNA EXONEREE

Guards are dragging Kirk Bloodsworth down a brightly lit hall. He's wearing an orange prison suit. His hands and feet are cuffed. He's kicking and screaming. He trips and falls. The guards roughly drag him to his feet. They lead him to the gas chamber. Once inside, he is strapped down.

"But I'm innocent!" he keeps screaming. No one listens. He gasps for air. He feels the world closing in on him.

Then he wakes up. He is drenched in sweat. He has had the nightmare again.

Wrongly convicted, Kirk Bloodsworth was imprisoned for nine years.

Kirk Noble Bloodsworth was freed in 1993 after nine years in prison. Two of those years were on death row. A DNA test proved he was innocent all along. To this day he continues to have nightmares.

A Failed Justice System

Sometimes the U.S. justice system fails. Courts can be wrong. They may convict an innocent person. Kirk Bloodsworth is just one of many. He was tried and convicted for a crime he didn't commit. The court sentenced him to die in the Maryland gas chamber. Eventually DNA evidence proved he was innocent.

Bloodsworth became the first death row inmate *exonerated* by DNA evidence. The governor of Maryland pardoned him. Eventually he was awarded $300,000. Most of it went toward his legal bills.

Despite his exoneration, many people still thought he was guilty. Employers wouldn't hire him. A woman saw him and screamed, *"Child killer!"* This was *after* DNA evidence had proven him innocent. Other *exonerees* have had similar problems.

Arrested for Child Rape and Murder

In 1984, Kirk Bloodsworth had just gotten out of the Marines. He had been honorably discharged at age 23. After that he went back home to Maryland. He was married. He had no criminal record. He worked as a crab fisherman.

On July 25, 1984, a little girl was found brutally murdered. Dawn Venice Hamilton, age 9, had lived in Rosedale, Maryland. She wore a pageboy haircut. She had a gap-toothed smile. Her body was found in the woods near her home. She had been beaten with a rock, raped, and strangled.

Investigators collected evidence at the crime scene. Police began the search for a suspect. Two weeks later they arrested Bloodsworth. A tipster had called police without leaving a name. Several witnesses said they saw Kirk with Dawn shortly before her murder. There was no physical evidence linking him to the scene.

The court convicted Bloodsworth and sentenced him to death.

A Flawed Case

There were problems with Bloodsworth's case. All of the evidence was *circumstantial*. And there was *exculpatory* evidence about another suspect. This evidence could have cleared Bloodsworth. But it was not presented in court.

Several children had seen a stranger offer to help Dawn find her cousin. A police sketch artist drew a picture of the suspect. The artist based the picture on the children's descriptions. The sketch was published in newspapers and shown on TV. Someone called the police and said it looked like Bloodsworth.

Misidentification is the chief cause of false imprisonment. DNA has exonerated more than 200 people so far. Of these, 75 percent were wrongly convicted by misidentification. There are many reasons why this happens. There are even scientists who study misidentification. They try to find out why eyewitnesses are often wrong.

But Who Really Did It?

Bloodsworth got out of prison in 1993. It was another 10 years before police caught the real killer. Bloodsworth was tired of people not believing him. He kept reminding authorities that the real killer was still out there.

Finally, in 2003, the court ran the crime-scene DNA through CODIS. The DNA test identified the real killer. It was a man named Kimberly Shay Ruffner.

Ruffner confessed to the crime after DNA proved him guilty. Strangely, he had been at the same prison as Bloodsworth for five years. The two men knew each other. Ruffner was a violent sex criminal. He was in prison for another crime. Ruffner knew Bloodsworth was innocent because he was the real killer. But he never told authorities.

Nine Years of Hell

The nine years Bloodsworth spent in prison were pure hell. He had been sentenced to die in Maryland's gas chamber. At his trial, people cheered when the verdict was read. They thought the court had convicted a little girl's killer. But they were mistaken. He was the wrong guy.

Bloodsworth was treated cruelly in prison. Everyone thought he was a child rapist and killer. Child abusers are at the bottom of the ladder in jail. Guards and other prisoners were very rough on him. Several times he nearly lost his life.

At one point the court granted him an *appeal.* A new trial was held. He lost again. But his death sentence was changed to two life terms.

Bloodsworth read everything he could. He learned all about law. At the time, DNA testing was new. He tried to convince his lawyer to get it done. He knew it would prove his innocence. But it was an uphill battle. People didn't know much about DNA testing then.

Finally, he convinced authorities to DNA test the crime-scene evidence. They compared it to his DNA. The test proved he was not the killer. On June 28, 1993, he was released from prison.

A New Life

Bloodsworth struggled for years after his release. He didn't want to talk about his time in prison. It was too painful.

These days he wants everybody to know his story. He speaks at schools and other public arenas. He tells people that if it could happen to him, it could happen to them too.

Today he works for the Justice Project. This group fights against the death penalty. They also address wrongs in the criminal justice system. They educate the public about injustices in the U.S. legal system.

CHAPTER 4

LIFE AFTER DNA EXONERATION

DATAFILE

T I M E L I N E

December 2, 1985

A Philadelphia woman is raped. She later points out Vincent Moto as her attacker.

September 21, 1994

Texan Gilbert Alejandro is freed after forensics "expert" Fred Zain is proven to be a fraud.

June 17, 2003

Ken Wyniemko is released after almost nine years in a Michigan prison.

Where is Clinton Township, Michigan?

KEY TERMS

expunge—to erase or remove from official records

false imprisonment—the unlawful restriction of another person's movements

settlement—money offered to settle a lawsuit without going to court

statute of limitations—a law limiting how much time can pass before a crime can no longer be prosecuted

stigma—a symbolic mark of shame or disgrace

DID YOU KNOW?

Forensics "expert" Fred Zain died of cancer in 2002. He was 52. Zain had repeatedly lied on the stand about DNA tests. As a result, West Virginia and Texas had to pay out a lot of money to wrongfully convicted persons.

LIFE AFTER DNA EXONERATION

"DNA is God's signature. It's never a forgery, and His checks don't bounce."
—DNA exoneree Eddie Joe Lloyd, 1948–2004

A Musician's Tale

Vincent Moto loves music. It's one thing that makes him feel better about life. His hip-hop song "After Innocence" tells his painful story. The song is featured in the movie of the same name. This film shows how tough life can be for those wrongly convicted. They are finally out of prison. But they face a whole new set of problems.

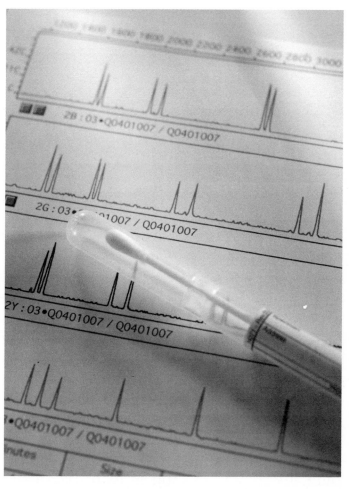

A DNA sample, like the one seen here, proved Vincent Moto's innocence.

And it's all because of crimes they didn't commit.

"It's ridiculous," Moto says. "They have programs for drug dealers who get out of prison. They have programs for people who really do commit crimes. People get out and go in halfway houses and have all kinds of support. There are housing programs for them, job placement for them. But for the innocent, they have nothing."

Moto's life turned upside down in 1985. One day he was walking down the street in Philadelphia. He was pushing his baby son in a stroller. Suddenly a woman pointed him out to police. She said Moto had raped her at gunpoint. The rape had taken place five months earlier. She was sure Moto did it. At least she thought so, anyway.

DNA evidence finally proved his innocence. By then Moto had spent over eight years in prison. After his release,

Pennsylvania did not apologize. Moto did not receive any money. The court did not even *expunge* his criminal record. The rape was not removed from his record. He was told it would cost $6,000 to have it removed. Without a clean record, he has a hard time finding work.

Exonerees Have a Stigma

Ken Wyniemko is from Clinton Township, Michigan. He used to manage a bowling alley there. Then he went to prison for nearly nine years. It was for a crime he didn't commit. DNA caught the real killer. Wyniemko was exonerated. But after that, he couldn't get a job anywhere. For two years, he applied for job after job. He applied for more than 100 in all. No one would hire him.

After years in prison, exonerees' job skills are out of date. They have huge gaps on their résumés. Some have never sent an email. Some haven't even typed on a computer. The horrors of prison can cause psychological problems. Exonerees often need counseling. They also need help with housing and transportation. But there are no state-run programs to help.

Exonerees seem to have a *stigma*, Wyniemko says. A stigma is like an invisible mark of shame or disgrace. Even though exonerees are innocent, they've been in prison. That scares people, including employers.

The Wrong Man

Wyniemko was imprisoned in a case of mistaken identity. A man broke into a woman's bedroom. He had a nylon stocking over his head. He sexually assaulted the woman. She later told police the rapist was between 20 and 25.

Wyniemko was 43 at the time. The victim didn't get a good look at the rapist because of the stocking over his head.

DNA testing was not yet available when Wyniemko went to trial. But blood tests proved he was not the rapist. He still went to prison. A prison snitch, Glen McCormick, helped put him away. McCormick now admits he made up the story. The prosecutor had promised him a deal for lying about Wyniemko.

Wyniemko had been in prison for nearly nine years. DNA testing finally came to his rescue. It proved that Craig Gonser was the real rapist. But the *statute of limitations* had run out. The court could not prosecute Gonser.

After Wyniemko got out of prison, he was out of work and out of luck. These days, though, things are looking better for him. He won a $3.7 million *settlement* and plans to go to law school.

An Expert Liar

Gilbert Alejandro spent four years in prison for rape. Most DNA exonerations are for rape and/or murder cases. That's because bodily fluids left at the crime scenes can be DNA tested.

The victim in this case told police a 6-foot-tall Hispanic man had raped her. She said he was wearing a white cap, gray T-shirt, and dark shorts. Police questioned such a man shortly afterward. But they made no arrest. Instead, several months later they arrested Alejandro. The victim had picked his photo out of a police mug book.

Alejandro went on trial. Forensics expert Fred Zain took the stand. He said Alejandro's DNA matched the DNA found at the scene. It didn't matter that the victim had failed to identify Alejandro in photo lineups. The court sentenced Gilbert Alejandro to 12 years in prison.

Four years later he was set free. It turned out Fred Zain had lied. *He hadn't even tested the DNA at all.* Zain wasn't even qualified to work as a forensics specialist. He had flunked organic chemistry. Zain had faked his way up the ranks in West Virginia, then in Texas. He had become a forensics star. Prosecutors loved him. He always provided the "right" conclusion on the stand: guilty.

Finally, the West Virginia Supreme Court investigated Zain. The report concluded that the guilt of 134 people was in doubt. Their convictions were based on Zain's testimony. At least nine of these people have been freed so far. One of them, Glen Woodall, sued the state of West Virginia for *false imprisonment*. He received a $1 million settlement.

Meanwhile, Gilbert Alejandro won a $250,000 settlement in Texas. Now he is getting on with his life.

CHAPTER 5

THE INNOCENCE PROJECT

DATAFILE

T I M E L I N E

1992

The Innocence Project is founded.

1993

The first death row DNA exoneree is released.

April 2007

The 200th DNA exoneree is released.

Where is Corsicana, Texas?

KEY TERMS

acquitted—declared not guilty in a trial

overzealous—too excited, to the point of being willing to do something wrong to meet a goal

persecute—to harass or torment

prosecutorial misconduct—conduct on the part of a prosecutor that violates court rules or ethics

public defender—a lawyer provided at no charge to a person who can't afford one

DID YOU KNOW?

Barry Scheck and Peter Neufeld are cofounders of the Innocence Project. Both were part of O.J. Simpson's defense team. They helped get Simpson *acquitted* of murdering his ex-wife.

THE INNOCENCE PROJECT

"I am an innocent man, convicted of a crime I did not commit. I have been *persecuted* for 12 years for something I did not do."

Those were the last words of Todd Willingham of Corsicana, Texas. He said them right before he was executed on February 17, 2004. That was after spending 12 years in prison on death row.

A Sad Christmas Tale

Willingham's story began in 1991, two days before Christmas. He was 23 and had been laid off from his job. Stacy, his wife,

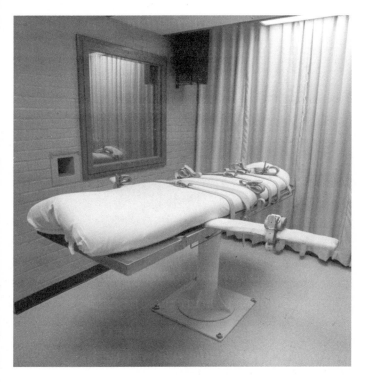

This table is fitted with restraints to hold down death row prisoners while they are being given a lethal injection in Huntsville, Texas. Todd Willingham was executed here in 2004.

worked at a bar. They had three little girls. Amber was 2, and twins Karmon and Kameron were 1.

That morning, Stacy had left to do some Christmas shopping. Todd was in bed when a fire broke out. He awoke to billowing black smoke. He heard cries of "Daddy! Daddy!" It was Amber.

He crawled along the floor under the thick smoke. He was trying to get to the girls' room. A burning ember fell and hit his shoulder. His hair caught fire. He panicked. So he turned and ran for the door.

The house burned down. Sadly, the three little girls died.

Several weeks later, police arrested Todd. The charge was triple murder. The court convicted him and sentenced him to death. Prosecutors said he had set the fire that killed his children.

Scientists later looked at the arson reports. They were full of mistakes. The fire inspector's methods were outdated. He hadn't proved the fire was arson at all. And he certainly hadn't proved that Willingham had done it. To the scientists, the fire looked like an accident.

Todd's cousin Pat took the scientists' evidence to Texas authorities. She tried to get the governor to stop the execution. But it was too late. Todd was dead.

Presumed Innocent

The *presumption of innocence* is a legal right in the United States. This means the accused is said to be innocent until proven guilty. In other words, prosecutors have to prove guilt. If they can't, the accused person must be set free.

Often it doesn't work that way. Sometimes the court sends innocent people to prison. There are many reasons. Racism is one possibility. African-Americans and Latinos have a higher conviction rate. But this may be because more are in poverty. Poor people can't afford high-powered lawyers.

Sometimes a poor person gets a *public defender*. That is a lawyer provided at no charge. Some public defenders are inexperienced. Sometimes they have a heavy caseload. With too many cases, they can miss important details.

Innocence May Not Be Enough

Innocent people often think the mistake will be cleared up quickly. So they tell police everything they know. They figure they did nothing wrong. They have nothing to hide.

But sometimes police just want to wrap up the case quickly. This is especially true when the crime is a sensational one.

The public wants to know what happened. Prosecutors pressure the police to find a suspect. When the case is "solved," the newspapers make the police look like heroes. And the public feels safe again.

So police sometimes lie to suspects. They may say there's strong evidence when there's none. Sometimes they beat suspects. Other times they deprive them of food, water, or sleep. Sometimes they force suspects to confess. Then police use the "confession" against the suspect in court.

Another reason for wrongful convictions is *prosecutorial misconduct.* That's when prosecutors get *overzealous* about doing their job. They want to win at all cost. So sometimes they withhold evidence. They mislead witnesses. They may also put prison snitches on the stand. Inmates will sometimes lie in exchange for a reduced sentence.

Bad science is a problem, too. The Todd Willingham case is far from unique. Forensics labs get pressure from prosecutors. So they cut corners. Sometimes evidence is handled incorrectly. Testing may be done with outdated methods. Forensics labs may be overloaded with too many cases. Sometimes technicians are poorly trained.

The Innocence Project

These are just a few of the problems that can make our court system unfair. As a result, many innocent people go to jail—or, worse, are executed.

Barry Scheck and Peter Neufeld decided to help. In 1992 they founded the Innocence Project. This organization works to change the justice system. The main thing they do is help innocent prisoners get DNA exonerations.

Many lawyers work with the Innocence Project. They help to correct an unjust system. Law students help the Innocence Project, too. They review thousands of prisoner letters. They help find innocent prisoners. They do legwork. Then the lawyers file appeals. They also request DNA tests. If needed, they represent the client in court.

Helping Exonerees

Getting help for DNA exonerees is also a priority. Some states don't offer them any help at all. In other states, prisoners can sue for financial compensation (money). Currently only 27 states offer compensation. In other states, such as Alaska, there is none.

A guilty prisoner out on parole often fares better than an innocent one. Parolees get health care and job and housing assistance. An exoneree gets none of these. The Innocence Project is changing that.

Another thing the Innocence Project does is work to preserve evidence. In some states evidence may be destroyed after a time. Without DNA evidence, an innocent person's case is often doomed.

Videotaping *interrogations* is also important. That's when the police question a suspect. Videotaping protects both sides. There may be a small detail that later becomes important. The taping catches it. It also keeps the police from having to take notes. They can concentrate on asking questions. The Innocence Project works on getting videotaping laws made.

The Innocence Project is working hard to fix the justice system. Thanks to its efforts, many Americans are changing their views on the death penalty, too.

GLOSSARY

acquitted—declared not guilty in a trial

chromosome—a threadlike body that carries genes

circumstantial—indirect, or of less importance

CODIS—Combined DNA Index System

database—a large, searchable collection of data, or information, kept in a computer

exculpatory—tending to clear of fault or guilt; usually describes evidence that proves innocence

exonerate—to officially clear someone of guilt or blame *after* he or she is convicted of a crime

exoneree—one who has been exonerated

expunge—to erase or remove from official records

false imprisonment—the unlawful restriction of another person's movements

familial—relating to family members

GLOSSARY

gene—the basic physical unit of heredity

genome—the full set of all the genetic traits people can inherit

helix—a three-dimensional spiral

infallible—absolutely sure or trustworthy

misidentification—to incorrectly identify someone

overzealous—too excited, to the point of being willing to do something wrong to meet a goal

persecute—to harass or torment

prosecutorial misconduct—conduct on the part of a prosecutor that violates court rules or ethics

public defender—a lawyer provided at no charge to a person who can't afford one

rape kit—a collection of evidence from a rape

settlement—money offered to settle a lawsuit without going to court

statute of limitations—a law limiting how much time can pass before a crime can no longer be prosecuted

stigma—a symbolic mark of shame or disgrace

suspect—a person the police think may have committed a crime

INDEX

INDEX